Published by:
Powder River Publishing LLC
1014 Black Mountain Road
Thermopolis, Wyoming 82443

Copyright © 2024
ISBN: 978-1-956881-40-0
Printed in the United States of America

No part of this publication may be reproduced, stored, transmitted in any form — electronic, mechanical, digital photocopy, recording, or other without the express written approval of the author.

All rights reserved solely by the author. The author guarantees all are original and do not infringe upon the legal right of any other person or work. The views expressed in this book are not necessarily that of the publisher.

All photography was used with the permission of the photographers and cannot be used, or reproduced without the express written permission of the publisher.

Dedication

Dedicated to my wife Carol and family, for their many years of love and support.

Special thanks to Ryan Collins, Carol Gagliano, Connor Gagliano and Carleen Cosner for the many beautiful photos, Julie Snyder and Janet Hansen for their help with my computer challenges, and Shawn Sullivan for his friendship and support.

Table of Contents

People

We Walked Together - 1
Little Boy - 2
The Most Important Thing - 3
Mama Cried - 5
Silk Bouquet - 6
Alive - 7
Baby's Checkup - 8
The Mailbox - 9
Airport - 10
Physical Therapists - 11
Special Friend, Special Place - 12
Compassion - 13
Fruit is Important - 14
Little Person - 15
The Barber - 16
Discarded - 17
Leftovers - 18
The Old Tree and Me - 19

Life

Waiting - 21
Slush Pile - 22
Broken Pottery - 23
Why? - 24
Today's Forecast - 25
Keys - 26
Smoke - 27
Strength - 29
Shroud of Dementia - 30
A Veteran's Pain - 31
Imagine - 32
After - 33
Disappointment - 34

Tornado - 35
Shades of Darkness - 36
Relief - 37
Blessings - 38
No Longer There - 39
Cereal - 40
Back Then - 41
Life emerges - 42
Two Red Eyes - 43
Invisible - 44
Friendship's River - 45
The Sky - 46
Mountain Wedding - 47
Flashback - 48
Doctor Says - 49
Tsunami of Pain - 50

Nature

Sunrise to Sunset - 52
December Sunrise - 53
Moonlight - 54
Snow and Wind - 55
Hidden Beneath - 56
March Thaw - 57
Silent Proclamations - 58
Close Your Eyes - 59
The River - 60
Rose - 61
Clear Creek Trail - 62
Sun, Shade and Shadow - 63
Bindweed - 64
A Ribbon of Peace - 65
Late Summer - 66
Summer's End - 67
Blackbirds - 68
Last Dance - 69
Lost in the Leaves - 70
October Snowstorm - 71
Gold and Silver - 72
Missing - 73
Kenai Hike - 74
My office windows - 75
Transition - 76
Tranquility - 77

People

We Walked Together

We walked in the sunshine
Laughed in the rain
Talked of the future
We both felt the same

We walked in the darkness
Searched for the light
Worked toward our goals
Our future looked bright

We walked in the good times
Hoped in the sad
Prayed for the strength
To get through the bad

We walked in to the future
Always with love
With strength from our God
In the heavens above.

Little Boy

The baby boy you once cradled in your arms,
grows to be a man.
He once looked up at you,
now you look up at him.
Your son once held your hand for safety,
now he shakes your hand.
You showed him how things worked
and now you ask him.
You see yourself in him strong, energetic, and confident.
He sees himself in you in time, weaker, less energy and unsure.
The little boy you loved so much, you love even more now.

The Most Important Thing

He wasn't tall in stature,
had a prominent Roman nose
and lost his dark brown hair early

His mother came over to America
at age four through Ellis Island
spoke broken English all her life

He grew up without a father
lost a little brother, forced to
live with one relative or another

Life made him tough
a fist fighter with a gentle heart
who loved to make people laugh

He didn't receive a high school diploma,
but was a certified diesel mechanic, learned
to play the guitar, base, piano and drums

He was a carpenter, electrician,
plumber, mechanic, musician
built his own home with a GI loan

He joined the army to serve his country
during World War II and wanted to
be a medic before a nervous breakdown

Fell in love and married, gave up
a career as a musician in a big band
for a beautiful Italian woman

He raised two sons, without a
degree in parenting and experienced
the loss of a daughter at birth

Always with a laugh and a smile
he did his best to live with depression
but was often hospitalized

Over his lifetime of seventy six years
he endured the pain and consequences
of several car accidents, none his fault

After fifty years of marriage renewed his vows
followed by a diagnosis of Alzheimer's
and hospitalization in a VA facility

In the end he became a shrunken
shell of himself, reminded me of
a featherless baby bird

In a lucid moment alone with him
teary eyed, he called me by my name
told me to remember

The most important thing is family.

Mama Cried

many years later
I know
why Mama cried

at my wedding
she shed tears of joy
but also tears
for the unknown future
ahead of my wife and I

Mama knew the joys
that lay ahead
must have remembered
the hopes she once had
on her wedding day

recalled the reality
of love's roller coaster
of raising a family
of heartache and broken dreams
cast upon her life

she knew the challenges
I would someday deal with
the good and the bad
she could no longer protect me
from the curves that life throws

many years later
I understand
why Mama cried

Silk Bouquet

A gift of his love
A silk bouquet of
Warm, wine colored
Roses, delicate but
Strong in sentiment

Everlasting
Much like a brilliant
Diamond, reflective
Of the eternal light
Of true affection

A grateful heart's
Desire to express
His deepest feelings
Like a lyrical song
That goes on forever

Alive

Woke up this morning
Oh, what a surprise,
I was still breathing
Could open my eyes.

Yawned and stretched
Stumbled out of my bed.
It must be a miracle
I wasn't dead.

My heart was beating
I still had a pulse,
My legs were working
If nothing else.

Put my hearing aids in,
My dentures in tight,
Adjusted my glasses
So I'd be all right.

Held on to my walker
Slipped on the floor,
Downed several pain pills
Then took a few more.

Used my inhaler
Now I could shout
Another great day
I'm up and about!

Baby's Checkup

Your baby appears to be exhibiting
signs of contentment and joy
as evidenced by his abundant
smiles and giggles.

His rosy cheeks, chubby hands and thighs
are a sign of robust physical condition.

Your baby's eyes sparkle with love and mischief,
observed by his keen interest
in checking everything out
I suggest you continue your regiment
of love and caring, to ensure his
continued growth and development.

The Mailbox

The widow cautiously shuffles out the front door toward the mailbox.

Hopeful there might be a card or letter from one of the children or grandchildren.

Worried she might discover an unpaid or overdue bill.

Excited there might be a colorful catalog or two to help pass the time.

Anxious that the mailbox might be empty.

The mailbox can make or break her day.

Airport

Inside the airport terminal
People scurry, human ants.
Outside small planes and jets
Buzz and swarm like bees.

A center for humanity
In all its diversity, brought
Together by travel technology.

Passengers anticipate destinations
All over the globe, unaware
Of the marvel of flight.

Physical Therapists

Men and women who set aside
Their own aches and pains to
Help others with theirs.

People who must endure
Watching others struggle through
Physical pain to help restore
Their well-being.

Physical therapists put their
Daily lives on hold
While they deal with the
Problems of their patients.

Special Friend, Special Place

My friend and I know
The Shack is a special place
that this time is a gift.

We share a bond with nature
appreciate its beauty,
strength and timelessness.

Quiet moments of reflection
deep thoughts shared, and laughter
create understanding and lasting friendship.

Memories of the adventure
precious in their simplicity
for us remain forever.

Compassion

visible in
smiles, hugs,
a shoulder pat,
serious focused listeners

why?

personal experience
accident, illness
loss of loved ones

born with it,
or modeled
taught by parents, religion

compassion,
reassurance that somebody cares

Fruit is Important

Mom says fruit is important.
That is why I use orange hand soap,
apricot body wash, raspberry shampoo
and blueberry hair conditioner.
I use cherry skin lotion, peach deodorant
and strawberry scented hand sanitizer.
Banana flavored gum is my favorite,
and I spray apple scented air freshener
in the bathroom.
Lemon scented hand lotion is a must, followed
by mango colored nail polish. And my favorite
clothes color is pineapple yellow.

Little Person

Life, born
from the womb
an infant
totally helpless

he or she breaths
sleeps and eats
relieves themself
cries for wants
and needs

nourished,
he or she grows
makes faces
eyes focus

hands and arms
coordinate
rolls over, sits up
teeth form

babbling sounds
become words
communication

crawls turn into
standing, walking
baby becomes
a toddler

a little person
emerges

The Barber

The barber
Not unlike a bartender
A sounding board
A counselor of sorts
Listens as he works
Patient, compassionate
Understanding
The person his client's trust
Aware of the lives of many

Discarded

Baby dolls and teddy bears
Tattered and torn
Tossed aside, thrown away
No longer loved or needed

Discarded

Automobiles and trucks
Rusted and contorted
Hauled away for parts
No longer working

Discarded

The elderly population
Life's worn and weary
Sent to nursing homes
No longer useful

Discarded

Leftovers

The refrigerator once
Filled with leftovers
From family and friends
Are almost gone.

Faded flowers wilt
And drop their petals
In scattered arrangements
Drying up around the house.

Sympathy cards lay
In a large pile of caring
On the dining room table
By his wife's picture.

The confused calico cat
Returns from hiding to
Be petted and snuggled
With her second-best friend.

The phone and doorbell
Now silent as the
Voices of loved ones
Echo in his mind.

The husband stares
At the oxygen tank
Lost in the memories

The Old Tree and Me

I stare at the old cottonwood
and remember. I see myself
once a sapling, strong and vigorous
my arms and legs limber and agile
like flexible tree branches reaching to the sky.

Its bark soft and smooth, now coarse
and scarred like my skin. The tree deeply rooted
where it was planted, and I rooted in the place
I chose to call home.

The tree has weathered many storms, and I
the trials and tribulations of life.

I see the tree's decline in broken branches
and bent trunk, mine is in arthritic gnarled fingers
and stooped back.

The tree isn't perfect, but neither am I, but
I do see a long life, a life like mine.

Life

Waiting

we wait for common everyday things
the mail to arrive, the coffee to brew
wait for seeds to sprout, flowers to bloom
tomatoes and sweet corn to ripen

we wait for important things
getting the needed job, a loan approved
wait for an illness to pass, medication to work
the doctor's call about the biopsy results

we wait for special things
summer vacation, a wedding day
wait for baby's first tooth, words, steps
holidays, birthdays and anniversaries

we wait for needed rain during drought
teens to come home after dates
wait for emails or packages to arrive
remodeling projects to be finished

we wait with patience or impatience
sometimes with trepidation, or uncertainty
wait with belief or unbelief
other times with excitement or joy

whether ordinary or important
we continue to wait, but
it's the delicate thread of hope
that keeps us waiting

Slush Pile

An editor's pile of dread
Or hidden treasure

A writer's source of
Anguish or joy

Like slush on the highway
It can change your destiny

Broken Pottery

Broken pottery waiting…

Much like me
a broken clay pot
lies empty and forgotten
tossed aside waiting
to be discarded and
thrown away

Once filled with
bountiful fragrant
colorful flowers
spilling over with
the joy of life
noticed and appreciated

Scorching sun, winds
heavy rain and hail
birds, insects and
clumsy people have
ruined a beautiful
living treasure

Much like me
once filled with
hopes and dreams
now broken
by harsh realities
and life's lessons

Broken poet waiting…

Why?

There are no words when a teen takes their life.

The shock is a nuclear bomb.

The emotional fallout toxic to the soul.

The debris is the loved ones left behind and

the trauma of "why?"

Anger, grief, and denial smolder in the ruins.

In time acceptance will rise from the ashes of love.

Today's Forecast

Today's outlook is for emotions
to be clouded with frustration
and possible outbursts of anger.

Lows may dip down to sadness
and disappointment, and highs
range from happy to exuberant.

The pressure will remain variable
throughout the day, causing problems to
blow in and exceed probable expectations.

Tomorrow's outlook is for more
of the same, with the addition of
a few scattered surprises.

Keys

There are keys to my house
Keys to my bike padlock
My safety deposit box
Keys to my luggage
To my office door
Keys to my safe
And my car
But the most important key
Is the one to my heart
My wife, who helps me find
All my misplaced keys.

Smoke

A shroud of sadness
engulfs our country
with smoke and ash
obstructs visibility
causing difficulty breathing
and air quality alerts

smoke searing sunsets
burnt offerings of a red sun
from the destruction and ruins
of devastating wild fires
fed by nature's evil side
of drought and winds

smoke like arid fog
dilutes blue skies
erases mountains
blots out panoramic vistas
and the long awaited
green freshness of summer

forests destroyed
communities obliterated
millions of minute particles
of human and animal remains
trees, and buildings
pollute the air we breath

smoke, lung's enemy
difficult to bear,
but nothing compared to
the unimaginable loss of life
family and friends
homes and businesses

treasured possessions, photographs,
souvenirs, irreplaceable
reminders of special memories
hopes and dreams dissolved
destroyed by heartless flames
the harbinger of death

smoke carries the irritants
that physically stress
the human heart and lungs
burns and blurs eyes
evokes sadness, fear, and anger
hopelessness and doubt

hope cremated by nature
becomes smoke, the incense
of loss and confusion
distorts our vision of the future
casting a gray haze of
doubt on the beauty of life

Strength

Strength is the widow who faces
another day without her spouse.
The man or woman who attaches
an artificial limb or gets back into a wheelchair.
The blind person or the burn-scarred
victim who goes out into public.
The depressed individual who takes
their meds and heads to work.
The cancer patient who leaves
for another chemo or radiation treatment.
The person who has lost
a loved one, or a home to fire or flood.
The recovering patient who faces
another session of painful physical therapy
or stressful counseling.
Athletes who resume hours of training, musicians, and dancers.
Policeman, fireman, doctors and nurses, therapists, EMTs, and teachers,
who set aside their own problems and pains to help people.

Shroud of Dementia

Remember,
your mother's love
dwells deep within her heart and soul.
It may be hidden, smothered
by the shroud of clouded confusion
of Alzheimer's
that masks her true feelings for you.

Yet, like the sadness of an overcast sky,
a ray of sunshine can often break through,
or like the bright yellow crocus of spring
can suddenly emerge, surprise you,
burst into bloom, and warm your heart.
May you be blessed with a moment
of her clarity, recognize, and treasure it.

Focus on the unconditional love she gave you,
continue to love her the same, and be at peace.

A Veteran's Pain

Read his poetry, felt the pain
His words bled off the pages
Wanted to reach out, let him know
I appreciated his sacrifice
Wished I could lessen his guilt, his hurt
Wanted to console and understand

War wounds ravaged his soul
Trauma still festered inside
Would despair and depression
Always shadow and haunt him
Would evil's poison turn him septic
Beyond help and recovery
Nightmare demons always taunt him
Are memories of war ever forgotten

Imagine

If God made the sun
and morning sun
can illuminate
dry dead grass

Imagine
what God can do
with our souls
when we die

Imagine

After

After the loss of a loved one,
knowing they're gone,
feeling sad, empty, aimlessly
going about daily routines
thinking you'll never laugh again
almost resenting life
for going on without them
there comes a moment

an inescapable something happens
a child hugs you, a friend stops by,
a flower blooms, or a bird sings
the flickering flame of hope returns
life won't be the same, but
you will experience happiness
and be grateful for the time
you had with your loved one.

Disappointment

Life has many disappointments
Intentional or not
They hurt, sometimes scar
Especially when it's a friend

Reasons may be valid
You never really know
What's going on with people
Even if you're close to them

If it's someone you love
You want them to be honest
And you try to understand
Because you care

Disappointment may be caused
By unrealistic expectations
You're not perfect, you forgive
And forget, they're still your friend.

Tornado

I watch it on the news
The aftermath of a tornado
Seated warm and comfortable
I try to imagine the personal loss

People wander like zombies
Amidst the carnage
Faces radiate disbelief
Rummage through the debris
Of their lives
Chilled by the cold
And emptiness of total loss

Family photos strewn like confetti
Among the bodies of loved ones
Neighbors and friends
The town obliterated in moments

Shades of Darkness

Darkness is not just the absence of light.

Darkness can be fear.
Common fears are those of spiders, snakes,
Crowds, needles, water, and heights.
We fear natural disasters, like earthquakes, tornados,
Hurricanes, blizzards, and wildfires.
We are afraid of losing our eyesight or hearing,
Physical abilities, or normal functioning.
The loss of a home, business or job, social position,
Or reputation is difficult to accept.
The loss of memory to dementia is a heart wrenching darkness.
The universal fear is that of death of self or loved ones.
The darkest of all fears is the loss of hope.

Darkness is not just the absence of light.

Relief

We all have that desk top,
junk drawer, or closet
that needs our attention.
Full, cluttered, unorganized,
they haunt us like a dark memory,
a heavy wet coat dragging us down,
keeping us from dealing with the problem.

If we emptied or cleaned it out
tossed the broken, useless and unnecessary
discarded all but the most sentimental
we'd find relief; life would be easier.
Why do we ignore and procrastinate?
One day, we finally face the lifeless demon
find relief, and wonder why we waited so long.

Blessings

She watched over you while here on earth
Cared and nurtured you from birth
Now she watches from above
With that special gift of a mother's love.

No Longer There

He awakens
Reaches over
But she's not there

Turns
Looks out the window
A single tarnished leaf
Clings to a skeletal branch

No song birds greet him
The sun's gone blotted out
By an unwanted profusion
Of somber clouds

Reality sets in
She's no longer there.

Cereal

I eat my cereal every morn
whether it's wheat, rice, oats or corn.
Peanut butter, strawberry, chocolate or more
so many flavors on the shelves at the store.

All kinds of shapes for goodness sakes
squares, circles, puffs, letters, and flakes
Enriched with vitamins, minerals too
with natural fiber, they're good for you.

Back Then

You didn't talk about it,
too young to understand
they said, so no explanation
act as if it never happened,
like it would really go away
with aunts hysterical and crying

but I saw my mother
sitting up in the hospital bed
arms reached out to me
tears welling up behind a dam
of unimaginable pain
her only words I lost the baby.

What did that mean? How? Why?
Nobody would explain it to me,
yet I'd just seen my first premature baby
a girl, my new cousin who
wasn't supposed to be born
but my sister was and she was gone.

Don't talk about it, help her
to forget, go on. Then one day
not long after, while cleaning
Mom found a mint green baby bonnet
she'd knitted, behind the corner
of the couch, and the ghost of sorrow
brought the tears again.

Life emerges

Fall planted bulbs poke green spears through thawed ground and
grow in to blazing red tulips and shy yellow daffodils. Millions
of dormant fruit tree buds burst forth a profusion of white and pink blossoms.

Morning angel sun arises from the black cloak of night, to shed light on a new day,
as a patient awakens from the dark depths of a coma.

Butterflies emerge from cozy cocoons and spread their ballet wings for flight, as
silvery jets sear through ominous clouds above. Below a ship sees a light house appear through the fog.

A surgeon frees someone from the misery of cancer, as a patient pushes through therapy to regain
mobility, and a cochlear implant restores hearing from a silent world.

Spring lifts itself from winter's grasp, as desert rainfall brings forth cactus flowers, and a new
life emerges from a mother's womb.

A blue whale surfaces from the cobalt ocean, as stars come to light through the mantle of night and
bats spiral forth from the cold blackness of a cave.

The truth becomes apparent with evidence, as education transpires into knowledge,
and research becomes a cure.

Life emerges.

Two Red Eyes

Two red eyes fade
into the predawn darkness
of the highway and vanish
like something alien.

Drivers headed to work,
maybe oil field workers,
or the DJ from the local radio station
getting ready to share
the weather report or local news.
Might be a school bus driver
needing to get an early start
picking up students in rural areas.

Perhaps it's the cook at the Busy Bee
who prepares breakfast for the night shift,
or the baker from Lolly's
who will knead dough for today's cinnamon rolls,
or the gal at the Quick Stop
who brews coffee for truckers.

The two red eyes are the people
who help start our day.

Invisible

You can't see panic,
electrical static
arcing inside
pulsing, coursing through
every vein and artery
yet it's there,

you know it's there
chains that bind you
rope that tightens
threatens your very being

but they don't see it
they can't see it

invisible to them
like air

if they could perceive it

would it make a difference?

Friendship's River

Friendship is like two streams that
join and become a powerful river.
They share life's journey.
Help each other to keep moving.
Support each other when the log jams
of disappointment and loss change their course.
Strengthen each other in the rapids of change.
Laugh and enjoy each other's company
when the water flows smoothly.
True friendship is a beautiful gift,
Like a river that helps sustain life.

The Sky

Always there,
Ever changing
Like me

Sometimes bright
Sometimes dark

Sometimes clear
Sometimes clouded

Feeling close
Feeling distant

Hopeful sunrise
Discouraged sunset

Relaxed and calm
Agitated, nervous

Warm colored
Dismal gray

Always there,
Never the same
Like me

Mountain Wedding

Outside on a mountain top
overlooking Meadowlark Lake
in the Big Horn Mountains
a young man, a former student
and his beautiful fiancé
stood facing each other
in a gentle breeze
before the pastor
repeating their sacred vows

Two young lovers
blending different cultures
together with love
sharing hopes and dreams
of a bright future

As I watched the couple
someone in front of me
pointed off to the side
where two eagles gracefully
emerged from a soft blue horizon
soaring from two directions
on warm summer thermals

Approaching each other
they joined together
flew off as a pair
disappearing in to
the distant unknown
a sign from above
as the bride and groom
completed their vows

Flashback

Alone on the walking path
I pass by the bridge
Nestled among the cottonwoods
A peaceful spot with
An invitation to peek
At the clear rushing stream below
And sooth my soul

But this time I have
A flashback to my youth
And another bridge
With a sense of dread and fear

My high school years
When I walked home
And had to cross a bridge
Over the muddy, polluted Cayuga Creek
Where a gang of teenage boys
Used to stop my crossing
Call me names and shove me around

Strange, after all these years
The memory of those altercations
Still surface and trouble me
Would I let that happen now?

Doctor Says

I used to love to eat
And never worried about
What or how much food

Now, my doctor says
I need to limit my salt intake
Not good for my blood pressure

My doctor says
I need to watch my caloric intake
It will put on the pounds

He says I must control
My protein, potassium and phosphorous
Bad for my kidneys

The doctor says I should
Limit my red meat meals
Too much iron not good for a man

Doc says control your sweet tooth
Too much candy, cookies, cakes and pies
And I might end up with diabetes

My doctor says take in lots of fiber
Nuts, grains and leafy greens
But too much and I'll have the runs

The doctor says to avoid
Caffeinated tea and coffee
It will mess with my irregular heart beat

Waiter asks, "What can I get you, Sir?"
"I've decided I'm not very hungry.

Tsunami of Pain

In the black hole of darkest night
It awakened me from a deep sleep
An unsuspecting, uninvited, physical intrusion
It forcibly struck,

A cranial attack

Sledge hammer pounding
Tsunami of pain
One crushing wave after another
An invisible electric arc
From my left eye to my ear
A relentless torture of agony

Leaving me helplessly weak
And nauseated

Another migraine

Nature

Sunrise to Sunset

We awake each day
to continue life's journey
not knowing what influence
nature will have on it
unaware of how people
will affect our lives

Minute by minute,
we live hopeful,
as if life is forever
conscious of the fact
that death is eminent
and fate holds our destiny.

December Sunrise

Sometimes my thoughts
Get tangled in the bare
Winter boughs.

I see through my window
The intricate tapestry
Woven into the winter sky.

A mural of natural beauty
Flooded with ribbons of mauve
Rich rose and royal gold.

Color inflames the horizon
Backlighting the early sunrise
Of a frigid December morning.

I'll strive to capture
This precious scene in a painting
Knowing the impossible.

Moonlight

the moon embedded
in the black satin sky
surrounded
by strands of ermine clouds
cast blue light
on the snowy
wedding white quilt below

moonlight reflects
off the rhinestone flakes
like twinkling stars
woven into the wintry cover

frosted spider webs
appear as lace
icy capped peaks
wear silver crowns
a frigid frosty
winter night's
cold mirage of beauty

Snow and Wind

Angel white snowflakes
Delicately crocheted into
A myriad of patterns
Gracefully descend
Like lacey curtains
A mysterious illusion
Of tranquil beauty

Until the cold brutal
Bully wind deliberately
Confronts its beauty
With jealousy and anger
Sweeping the veil away
Into suffocating clouds
Obstructing everything

Evil birth of a blizzard

Hidden Beneath

Out the window
The garden appears lifeless
Except for the green of junipers

The gray angel statue stands
Solemnly waiting for spring
A quilt of freshly fallen glitter
Protects the life hidden beneath

I miss the yellow chiffon of daffodils,
The perfume scented purple iris
The warmth of peach-colored roses,
And beauty of each new blossom.

In my heart lies the seed of hope
Until winter ends and so
I cultivate patience until spring.

March Thaw

Trickling rivulets of icy water
Meander down roadside banks
Glassy pools and puddles shimmer
Reflect azure blue March sky
Moisture revives almond grasses to green
The never-ending promise of spring beckons

Silent Proclamations

Golden daffodils trumpet the arrival
Ruby tulips roll out the red carpet
Lavender lilacs sweeten the welcome
A silent, powerful proclamation of spring

Close Your Eyes

Close your eyes and listen

The canopy of leaves
The creaking branches
The endless wind, but
you will not hear
my dying heart

Close your eyes and listen

A riveting flicker
Chipmunk chatter
The gurgling stream, but
you will not hear
my suffocating soul

Close your eyes and listen

The honey bees' hum
The restless rustling grasses
The sparrow's song, but
you will not hear
my fleeting hope

Close your eyes and listen

The River

The river is life,
at times tranquil and placid
lulls you into a sense of peaceful trust
yet beware of hidden snags beneath
the dark eddies shaded by trees
that precariously cling to the waters' edge.

Spring runoff torrents scour and
ravage the shore eroding and littering
it with tree carcass log jams.
Water swirls and slithers around rocks
boulders, bubbles silver white, winding
like liquid glass, it glides through forest shadows.

Rock and stone spattered shoals
host willows and wild flowers.
The banks sport frogs, otters and bear.
Ducks, herons and cranes navigate its curves.
Sieves, divide water as it slips and slides
and passes underneath double rocks.

It's a long continuous bending ribbon
of rhythm, gurgling and splashing
a musical melody of life racing, seeking
allowing nothing to stop its journey of song.
Obedient only to the laws of gravity, the river
is a harmony of ripples, rivulets, rapids, and waves.

Rose

Beautiful cannot describe the perfection of a rose
Velvet cannot describe its textured petals
Perfume cannot describe its ethereal scent
Words cannot describe its essence

A rose is the ultimate floral creation

Clear Creek Trail

A place to replenish the spirit
Let worries flow into the water
To float away or
Let stress rise into the canopy
Of cottonwood leaves

A place to think
To hear your inner voice
Find yourself again or
Appreciate the sights and sounds
Of nature's beauty all around

A place to visit friends and neighbors
Walking their dogs, riding bikes
Meeting new people or
A reprieve from the everyday
Noise that surrounds us.

Sun, Shade and Shadow

Sun, shade and shadow
Artists' tools to create
Depth in a painting

Sun fashions shade
That cools and visually
Softens a landscape

Sun enhances cottonwood leaves
To glisten as if laden with dew
Sparkling in the canopy

Sun fabricates intricate patterns
Of shadowed branches and leaves
On paths and roadways

Sun works with shade
To darken edges along the stream
Protection for trout

Sun fashions shade
In the trees and grasses
And shade invokes mystery

Sun, shade and shadow
A trio of creators
Working together with light

Bindweed

As a child
I used to see them
Growing along the roadside
Little delicate white bell flowers
Sprinkled on long green vines
Entwined on fences or tall stems of grass
Always happy to see them
Thought they were wild morning glories

As an adult
I still see them
Growing in my yard
Little delicate white bell flowers
Sprinkled on long green vines
Entwined on my fence and lawn
Choking my flowers and vegetables
Never happy to see them
Know they are not morning glories

A Ribbon of Peace

A ribbon
Of clear
Winding water
Glides
Caressing the earth
Slithers silently
Among emerald green
Wild iris reeds
Seeking shelter
In the shade
Of tired cottonwoods

I am drawn
To its tranquil
Slowly swirling
Rhythm
Lost in its clarity
A ribbon of peace
In a chaotic world

Late Summer

A spattering of yellow leaved willow
mimic the late summer golden rod.
The panoramic mountains, veiled
in smoke from distant forest fires
sparked by dry thunderstorms
appear like a landscape mirage.

The forest is shrouded in shades of green
spruce, pine, and fir. The larch
soon to turn vivid yellow
and drop their needles.
Pastel purple lemon-eyed asters
peek through weathered grasses.

White washed skeletal trees
baked and bleached by the sun
that once gave them life, are
reminders of raging spring runoff
cling to the eroding river banks.

A lone plane punctuates the
lingering haze of August sky
with an amplified buzz.
A bald eagle, monarch of the river
searches for prey, ready to swoop
down on the unsuspecting.

The refreshing joy of spring
forgotten. The land prepares for
summer's final curtain and
autumn's colorful debut.

Summer's End

I rest outside by the front flower garden
in my black metal swing chair
listening to the melodic babble of the fountain.

The once slender sapling aspen
stares down at me from its emerald canopy,
trembling at the thought of summer's end.

Hot and dry the last lilies trumpet in defiance at the sun,
as roses are ruined by their serrated petals
altered by cutter bees.

Purple petunias bedraggled by grasshoppers, hail and wind
continue to bloom defying hostile August.

Finches cluster around the feeder and bees vibrate
among the mums and asters in their finale.

Like a ghost, a mule deer passes by
alert, ears twitching unaware of my sadness
at summer's end.

Blackbirds

Blackbirds, beads of ebony
Decorate power lines
Flutter in waves of motion
Transparent black clouds

Careless winds rape
The splendor of October leaves
Decked out in scarlet
Lemon and tangerine attire

A lingering sun
Bleaches the skeletal
Prairie grasses that
Jostle in the breeze

Summer dreams have
Dried up in the heat
And drought, evaporated
Into wildfire smoke

Last Dance

Water in the stream hurries south
afraid to be left behind to freeze.
Birds gather in feathery flocks
creating dark waves on the horizon.
Clouds come together and suffocate
blue sky and turn it to gray.
Northwest winds dry grass stems
into slender brown skeletons.
Clematis vines envelop bushes
with frothy looking bearded seed pods.
Trees show their true colors
and let leaves have one last dance
a waltz with the wind as they flutter
colorfully down to earth and die.

Lost in the Leaves

When leaves show their true colors
I get lost in the leaves of autumn

Gold dripping from the weeping birch
Magenta Virginia Creeper vines
Draped over trees and shrubs
Chokecherry bushes flaunting carmine, orange, and yellow

Ash trees brilliant goldfinch yellow
Aspens fluttering lemon coins
Cottonwoods bedecked in leaves like gold doubloons
Maples in apple red, autumn orange, and sassy yellow

Apple and crabapple trees festooned in cranberry and copper
Cherry trees adorned in ruby, coral, and goldenrod
Burning bush afire with vibrant red foliage
Other trees speak of burgundy, bronze, and tangerine

Autumn leaves are a carnival of rich colors
A festival for the artist palette

October Snowstorm

Muffled
The earth is smothered
In cumulative snow
The breath of green grass
And helpless green leaves
Suffocate in the cold
White cloak of an early
Winter snowstorm.
The warmth of the solar star
Forgotten. The daunting landscape
Hides the remains of autumn's glory.

Gold and Silver

Early sunrise turns
the empty trailer windows
on the side of the hill
a coppery gold

The pond's polished surface
ripples reddish gold
sparkles like precious jewels

Champagne colored light
cloaks a field of dried grass

Pine needles appear almost metallic
as early rays filter through

Rocks shine glossy wet
driftwood becomes white bones

Later the pond's surface
shimmers with silver light
but the windows lose their
magical beauty

Missing

I miss the simplicity of The Shack
the serenity of its isolated location
the black spruce etching against the sky
the downy snowflakes without the wind

I miss the warmth of Muck boots and long johns
and the crackling fire in the wood stove
the hot tea with honey in the morning
the long conversations at night

I miss the view from the windows
the moonlight on the forest
I miss the teasing and laughter
I miss Salmon, his lovable dog

I miss the simple meals
the walking to and from The Shack
the anticipation of seeing the northern lights
and the security of a good sleeping bag

But most of all, I miss the
uninterrupted time with my friend.

Kenai Hike

We decided to hike around the property
surrounding The Shack in the Alaskan bush.
Twenty- to twenty-four-inch-deep heavy wet snow
made the hike challenging. Soft gray skies and mist
nestled over us, as we trudged among the thick forest of black spruce.
Hidden beneath a white mantle, steps collapsed into pools of water,
the bloated soil ready to suck our boots into itself.

Smaller spruce grew in snow drifted clusters, frozen prisoners until spring thaw.
The evergreens thinned as they fanned out into the vast meadow lost to the horizon.
Moose, marten, and lynx wove chains of tracks among the landscape.
Spiny stems of Devil's Club rose from mounds of snow ready to inflict their sting.
Ravaged crowns of six-foot cow parsnip, once a summer's glory,
stood, tilted, tattered, and torn in swaths of brittle skeletal remnants.
Layered fringes of fungus created ladders up birch trunks,
and a few reluctant cranberries clung to bare branches like rubies.
A lone sparse tamarack tree stood laced in delicate amber needles, as
two friends embraced the winter cold to see the beauty of Alaska's winter.

My office windows

Look out
Over the plains and foothills
Of Wyoming
The bison herds
Have been replaced
By herds of black angus
No teepees the on the prairie
Housing developments devour the land
Gravel pits gauge out pastures
Making miniature manmade foothills
The expanse of blue skies is
Marred by floating jet trails
Bird song mixes with the sounds
Of trucks and cars on highways
Wagon trains no longer traverse trails
Interstate highways speed semi-trailers
Smaller herds of deer and antelope
Still graze on the disappearing grasslands
Much has changed in the west
Except for one thing, the wind

Nothing can change the wind

Transition

rushing rapids
settled into ripples
wild iris leaves
frayed by hungry deer
stagnant pools of algae green
gold of sunflowers,
  golden rod, and sticky gumweed
royal purple of thistle
asters and gay feather
days shorten, shadows lengthen
summer slips away

Tranquility

Early morning
I search for meaning
in the spruce spires
adorned with snow.

Ethereal mist embraces
the canopy of conifers.
Snowflakes sift
through languid limbs.

Serenity is precious
in today's world.
Why is peace
so difficult to grasp?

My thoughts and memories
intertwine with the beauty
spread out before me
lost in Alaska's tranquility.

Author Biography

Known by many as the teacher who dances on his desk, Eugene M. Gagliano (pronounced Galiano) is a retired elementary teacher with a great sense of humor. He and his wife Carol, who have four children and seven grandchildren, live near the base of the Big Horn Mountains in Wyoming. Gene enjoys reading and writing, traveling, hiking, acrylic painting, singing tenor in the community choir, and spending hours flower and vegetable gardening. Gene's author presentations are entertaining, informative, and inspirational. He has presented at 184 schools, and at IRA, teacher, SCBWI, and library conferences, and for libraries and festivals in Wyoming, Colorado, Missouri, South Dakota, Minnesota, Montana, Nebraska, Texas and Hawaii. Gene was the recipient of the IRA's 2004 Wyoming State Celebrate Literacy Award and the 2001 Arch Coal Teacher Achievement Award. Gene's book Dee and the Mammoth illustrated by Zachary Pullen, won the 2010-2011 Wyoming State Historical Society Award for Best Fiction. *Dee and the Mammoth represented the state of Wyoming at the National Book Festival in Washington, D.C in 2011. His other books include C is for Cowboy, a Wyoming Alphabet; Four Wheels West, a Wyoming number Book (a former Western Writer's Spur Award nominee); V is for Venus Flytrap, a Plant Alphabet; My Teacher Dances on the Desk (winner of the 2010 Delaware Diamonds Book List Children's Choice Award); Secret of the Black Widow (a former Wyoming Indian Paintbrush Award nominee); The Magic Box; Falling Stars; Inside the Clown; Booger; Little Wyoming; Angel's Landing; Is It True? (2017 children's humorous poetry book); Snap (2019) 2nd place 2019 Evvy Award winner and Wedge of Fear (2018) 3nd place 2019 Evvy Award winner. He has two hard covers, beautifully illustrated in color poetry books, A Wyoming State of Mind (2021) and More Than Four Seasons (2022). He is a graduate of the Institute of Children's Literature, and is on the Wyoming Arts Council Artists Roster. Gene is the Wyoming State Poet Laureate Emeritus. His book Is It True? was selected as the state of Wyoming's Best Read for 2018 for the National Book Festival in Washington, DC. Gene's latest children's poetry book What Did You Say? (2021) is the sequel to Is It True?. Little Hawaii and My Veggie Friends (illustrated by Gene), are his most recent books, along with Secret of the Black Widow (his first middle grade historical fiction book) being rereleased with its new sequel Ice Cave Mystery. Gene has two new contracts, one for My Fruity Friends (a sequel) and an adult poetry hardcover book with color photos titled Sunrise to Sunset. The WY PBS released a documentary, in 2022, about Gene being the Wyoming Poet Laureate. Check out his website at www.gargene.com or his face book author page at www.facebook.com/dancingteacher.

List of Organizations: Society of Children's Book Writers and Illustrators, Wyoming Writers, Wyoming Poets, Johnson County's Arts and Humanities Council, Friends of the Library, and the Wyoming Arts Council.

Website: www.gargene.com

FB Author Page: www.facebook.com/dancingteacher

Author Page on Amazon: Amazon.com/author/www.gargene.com

www.ingramcontent.com/pod-product-compliance
Lightning Source LLC
Chambersburg PA
CBRC091203010526
44107CB00021B/1232